TOY TRAIN *Memories*

TOY TRAIN *Memories*

John Grams

KALMBACH
BOOKS

Acknowledgements

This is the place where people who have contributed significantly to the development of a given book are formally thanked for their participation and support. In the case of *Toy Train Memories,* such a task would be difficult at best, and because there are so many individuals to thank, someone would undoubtedly be left out. Besides, a long list of names—literally hundreds have been involved in some way—seems pointless. Most of those who contributed photos are identified with the stories, captions, or credits at the back of the book. I would like to expressly thank the hundreds of *Classic Toy Trains* magazine readers who generously took the time to comb through their family albums and then trusted the mail services to get their photos safely to us. Those captured moments of youthful joy are spectacular. Thank you all. And certainly, *Classic Toy Trains* editor Neil Besougloff and his staff deserve a hand for allowing us to use their archives and for getting the word out to their readers about this project so that we would have the photos necessary to complete the book. Your enthusiastic support of the book from the beginning is appreciated. Finally, thanks go to my good friend and colleague Dick Christianson, who edited this work. We spent many hours discussing the connection between Christmas and toy trains.

Printed in Canada

02 03 04 05 06 07 08 09   10 9 8 7 6 5 4 3 2 1

Publisher's Cataloging-in-Publication
Grams, John.
    Toy Train memories / John Grams. — 1st ed.
    p. cm.
    Includes bibliographical references and index.
    ISBN 0-87116-198-2

    1. Railroads—Models—History. I. Title.

TF198.G643 2002   625.1'9'09
                        QBI01-200524

625.19
GRA

Art Director: Kristi Ludwig

Lionel and American Flyer are registered trademarks of Lionel LLC, Chesterfield, Michigan. "Marx" and related logos are the property of Marx Toys Inc., Miami, Florida. MTH is a registered trademark of M.T.H. Electric Trains. "K-Line" is the property of MDK Inc.

Page 2: Kenneth Morley, Christmas morning of 1936 or 1937

Table of Contents

Preface

A toy train running around the Christmas tree has been an American tradition for almost a century. The photos in this book attest to the fact that Christmas trees and toy trains are strongly linked in the minds and traditions of many Americans. Although the trains themselves might not be the popular holiday gifts they once were, in a broader sense they have actually become an integral part of the seasonal scene. For instance, K-Mart's television commercials in 2001 featured a Christmas tree with blue lights on it (what else?) and a little freight train chugging merrily beneath it.

Toy trains are an accepted element in the magic of Christmas—as much a part of the decorations as mistletoe, holly, pine boughs, and twinkling lights. For many, a Christmas tree by itself seems barren, or at least not fully dressed, without an electric train wending its way around and through the brightly wrapped presents beneath it.

Personally, I can't remember a Christmas without a toy train involved in some way. The first one arrived at my house in time for my second Christmas. For the next fifteen seasons, an ever-expanding display occupied the space next to the tree. By that time, I had become a "scale" model railroader with a somewhat permanent layout in another part of the house. In my teenaged mind, "toy" trains were for kids—or for Christmas trees.

Years later, when my own family came along, I renewed the tradition. My daughter received her first Christmas train when she was just nine months old. She couldn't actually "play" with the thing, but she enjoyed watching it and cried when it stopped. Her holiday layout was augmented every year for the next ten. I suspect this represents a familiar pattern among many families. The idea that it just wouldn't be Christmas without a toy train in the scenario has been passed down from generation to generation.

Yet, in all that has been published about toy trains (an immensely popular subject these past twenty-five years), and in everything written about family Christmas traditions and home holiday decorations (which goes back even further), nobody has written a book that demonstrates the connection between the two.

Could the link between toy trains and Christmas be so natural, so obvious, so commonplace that everyone else overlooked it?

Apparently. That is how and why this book came into being. One result of this book's publication, then, is that it will fill a rather large gap in the literature of American popular culture. But more important, it is my simple wish that the photos and text in this book will rekindle warm and fuzzy memories of Christmases past and the toy trains that made them special to you or your loved ones.

—*John A. Grams*

The author got his start in toy trains in the 1930s with this O gauge set under the tree (top photo). Every year for the next fifteen the "under the tree" layout expanded until it went well beyond the shelter of the pine tree's boughs! When the author became a teenager he became a scale model railroader, but returned to his first love—toy trains—at his daughter's first Christmas. She was nine months old at the time! Today he's still actively involved in toy trains as a magazine writer, book author, and hobby observer. And every year he has a toy train under his tree.

Toy Trains from the Beginning

The first toy trains, crude wooden things designed to be pushed or pulled along the floor, appeared in the third quarter of the nineteenth century. Before long, manufacturers substituted cast iron for the wood because it was capable of capturing better detail. But the trains were still kid-powered.

Self-propelled trains that ran on sectional track came along in the waning years of the century, first developed by German and other European clock makers, who adapted their key-wound, spring-driven mechanisms for use in the toy field. To this day, trains that have to be wound up are usually referred to as "clockworks."

Toy train electrification came about slowly during the first two decades of the twentieth century. Although probably pioneered in Europe, by 1901, toy trains with electric motors in them were being manufactured on both sides of the Atlantic Ocean. Power for these early electric trains was supplied by primitive and often dangerous batteries. Reliable house current was available only in the major metropolitan areas. For most of the country, such a luxury was still a thing of the future.

The basic technology may have come from Europe, but American toy trains had a style and character all their own from the outset. This was due in no small way to the strong personalities of the men who captained the companies that produced them.

Lionel

Joshua Lionel Cowen, inventor and experimenter, had manufactured military hardware, developed a reliable electric motor, and worked on improving the dry-cell battery before he built the first Lionel train in his New York City loft in 1901. Actually, it was a motorized gondola car that ran on a circle of track, which he had intended to sell to storekeepers as an animated window display. Soon, people were playing with the thing, and a toy empire was born. Before long, Cowen was making a line of electrically powered trains and trolley cars.

Built largely upon the ingenuity of one man, who surrounded himself with a few well-chosen associates, Lionel became a powerful force in the American toy train market in the years after World War I. Cowen fought and eventually defeated most of his competitors, both foreign and domestic.

In spite of economic reversals during the Great Depression, Lionel emerged from the toy train production hiatus of World War II in a very strong position, the undisputed leader in the field. The golden age of Lionel trains followed. From the mid-1940s to the late 1950s, Lionel set standards in engineering and marketing that others could only hope to emulate. Profits soared. Annual sales numbered in the millions of units.

However, as J. Lionel Cowen's influence and leadership in the corporation eroded, so did product quality. When he retired in 1958, his son Lawrence became the figurehead chief executive, but stockholder groups fought each other for control. Cash flowed out of the company. To make matters worse, the toy train business was on the ropes in the 1960s, reflecting the diminished role of real railroads in American life. Kids wanted other kinds of toys. For Lionel Corporation, attempts at diversification came too late.

In 1969, the rights to manufacture trains under the Lionel trademark were granted to a subsidiary of General Mills. The cereal maker slowly turned the company around by changing marketing strategy and rebuilding the Lionel quality image. Instead of targeting children, the new Lionel made the adult collector its main focus. Old favorites from the 1940s and 1950s were reissued with new paint jobs.

Sixteen years later, Detroit real estate magnate Richard Kughn bought the business outright. He introduced state-of-the-art electronics and an array of newly designed trains to augment the golden oldies. Kughn, a life-long train enthusiast and collector found himself in the enviable position of manufacturing his own collectibles. Under his single-handed leadership, the line flourished for a decade.

Kughn sold the company to Wellspring Associates, an investment group, in 1995. The hundred-year-long heritage and classic tradition continue today under the supervision of Wellspring executives.

Ives

This Bridgeport, Connecticut, toy company had been in business for more than 30 years when it began marketing clockwork trains in 1901. The electric line came in about 1910. Ives was the first American firm to use colorful lithography extensively on their trains. Harry Ives, son of the founder, was at the helm when the train line was introduced. The Ives and Lionel lines were roughly equivalent in quality and price, so to compete, Ives offered little extras—a liberal trade-in policy and free factory service for life. These gestures built goodwill, but they cut deeply into the profit margin. Ives' insistence on never cheapening his products reduced profits even more.

Ives went bankrupt in 1928. The train interests were acquired by a coalition that included Lionel and American Flyer, and the two firms jointly produced Ives merchandise for the next two years. Then

Lionel bought out Flyer's share and moved production to the Lionel plant in Irvington, New Jersey. Cowen turned the Ives line into a new low-priced Lionel-Ives line. After two more years, he discontinued it.

American Flyer

Chicago hardware manufacturer William O. Coleman and mechanical toy maker William Hafner entered into partnership in 1907 to produce an inexpensive line of clockwork trains under the trade name "American Flyer." Hafner left in 1914 to set up his own train business, and the first American Flyer electrics appeared shortly thereafter. Although the company offered trains at all price levels, it acquired an economy-line image, which put it at a competitive disadvantage.

In 1938, A.C. Gilbert, who manufactured Erector sets, magic kits, and small appliances, bought American Flyer and moved it to his headquarters in New Haven, Connecticut. Gilbert switched the train line from O gauge to the slightly smaller S gauge in 1946. His scale models were attractive, well-made, and reliable performers, but because they were not compatible with the more prevalent O gauge trains, he garnered only about fifteen percent of the market. Gilbert's attempt to turn the toy train industry in his direction failed, and the company went out of business. Rights to the American Flyer name were acquired by Lionel in 1966. (A rather limited line of these trains was produced by Lionel in the 1980s and '90s.)

So, by the mid-1960s, Lionel had swallowed up two of its major competitors, American Flyer and Ives. However, it was not strong enough then to go after the one remaining—Louis Marx. The toy market had shifted, and Lionel found itself in the midst of a feverish attempt at diversification.

Marx

In the early 1930s, tin-toy maker Louis Marx obtained an interest in a company that manufactured cheap mechanical trains under the Joy Line brand. His own train line evolved from it. With inexpensive, durable windup and electric trains, Marx had a corner on the low end of the market almost immediately. His no-frills locomotives retailed for a dollar, his cars for a dime. Consumers liked the idea that they could put together their own sets *à la carte,* depending on what appealed to them.

Marx was the Henry Ford of the train business, offering products that were reliable and priced within reach of almost everyone. Although the original company went out of business in 1975, the train line was revived in the early 1990s. New Marx trains are currently available in a wide assortment of road names and colors.

Lionel's success in developing a new market among adult collectors and model railroad operators in the 1970s and '80s spawned a number of smaller specialized companies to service the same population. During the 1990s the adult version of the toy train hobby underwent a renaissance, and manufacturers and importers responded to the demand. MTH rapidly and aggressively introduced new products, offering full lines of trains, track, and accessories in two price ranges; they also offer reproductions of the large scale trains of the 1920s and '30s for the collector market. K-Line also provides a large array, from toylike sets to scale pieces. Atlas, Third Rail, Weaver, and Williams tend to focus on operators in search of realism.

Content and structure of the book

A note on relative popularity of the trains. This book does not intentionally discriminate among the various train manufacturers. The fact that Lionel trains seem to predominate is merely a reflection of the commanding market share the company enjoyed over the years, particularly in the period following World War II. American Flyer, though their apologists would argue, were a rather distant second in total unit sales.

The book that follows is loosely organized into six sections designed to give you a sense of the role toy trains played in the lives of children over the past century, in particular at Christmastime. Chapter One traces the origins of the connection between toy trains and Christmas from the beginning, through the golden years, and into the renaissance of the past two decades, when having a toy train running under the tree became an integral part of the greater Christmas tradition and a widely accepted item in holiday home décor.

Chapter Two focuses attention on the wildly anticipated wishbook catalogs, distributed every year by the train manufacturers, toy wholesalers, and retailers.

Chapter Three covers the gloriously whimsical holiday store-window displays, usually featuring at least one operating toy train to attract shoppers' attention and bring them inside.

Chapter Four moves to the in-store toy train layouts, many of which were quite lavish. Smart merchandisers usually positioned them in the toy department, next to the local Santa Claus, so kids would have something to divert their attention while waiting in line. While intended primarily as demonstrations for retail-toy buyers all year long, they became huge kid-magnets in December.

Chapter Five deals with toy trains in unrelated promotions of all kinds. This dates back to the very earliest commercial use of electric trains and continues to this day.

Chapter Six describes how toy trains were put to work in some popular holiday movies and, in particular, television shows over the years. It also aims the spotlight at some past and current celebrities who have embraced toy trains as a hobby.

Between chapters, you'll find a variety of classic photos of children enjoying toy trains on Christmas morning over the years. You'll also find an incredible variety of creative ways in which people continue to demonstrate that century-old intimate connection between toy trains and Christmas.

ONE

Christmas-Toy Train Connection
ORIGINS

Christmas and toy trains—one of those natural combinations that most Americans take for granted—like Thanksgiving and turkey, summertime and lemonade, Mom and apple pie. Over the past century, a toy train circling the tree has become an important element of traditional Christmas decoration in many American homes—even some of those that no longer have children living in them.

For a hundred years, families have enjoyed watching electric trains circle round and round their Christmas trees. Appropriately, a nativity scene often enjoys a prominent place within the circle of track, sharing the space with gaily wrapped packages. In some homes, elaborate Christmas villages occupy both sides of the track. Christmas just wouldn't be Christmas without a brightly lighted, glimmering evergreen; neither would Christmas be complete without a train beneath the tree.

Lionel published *Model Builder* magazine for more than a decade to promote the creative, year-around use of its trains in ways that emphasized realistic settings and operation, much like the adult-oriented scale model railroads that were springing up at the time. However, every December the magazine would go back to the roots and acknowledge the Christmas-toy origins of the hobby. This cartoon appeared in the centerfold of the last issue for 1947. It's a classic scene—the fulfillment of every boy's dream on Christmas morning, complete with Mom, Dad, the dog, and a large electric train layout under the tree.

Although it is fun to speculate, nobody knows for certain when and where the toy train was first associated with Christmas. That landmark event has been lost to history. It is easy to presume that it happened in the United States, but that too is not certain, perhaps unlikely.

Both windup and electric trains were produced in Europe first, and several German manufacturers, most notably Bing and Märklin, dominated the field prior to World War I. It was the wartime ban on these foreign imports that finally gave American firms such as American Flyer, Ives, and Lionel an advantage in the domestic market.

So, the tie between toy trains and Christmas may have initially come from Europe, along with some of our better Christmas carols. We don't know. However, once the idea took hold here, it soon became an American institution—like chop suey, pizza, and french fries!

Trains became favorite toys for boys (primarily) almost as soon as the real railroads were established. From crude wooden push toys, to wooden models with rolling wheels and lithographed paper sides, to cast iron pull trains, to live steamers, and finally to electrically powered models, toy trains have captured and held the attention of children for more than 150 years.

Not only did they capture the youthful imagination, they represented state-of-the-art science and cutting-edge technology. Electric toy trains were seen as educational toys that could help children understand the basics in the new field of electricity. It could even prepare them for careers in railroading—an expanding, almost glamorous industry at the time.

The secularization of the traditional display under the family Christmas tree also had a lot to do with connecting trains to the holiday season. Originally limited to the nativity and other religious scenes, these miniature dioramas were often quite elaborate and artistically done—something very special that appeared for a short time each year. Certainly, they were a big part of the magic and wonderment of the season, and the children loved them.

In some cultural or ethnic communities these displays became more secular as the years went by. Instead of representing events long ago in the Holy Land, they became pictures of recent or contemporary winter scenes closer to home. The Pennsylvania Dutch, for example, referred to them as "Christmas Gardens." Of course, Santa Claus fit in well with the whimsical, toylike demeanor of these gardens, many of which featured tiny villages as their central focus. It wasn't a long stretch to add a train and a circle of track to give motion and a dramatic new dimension to what had already become a holiday tradition.

Many people consider the 1930s as the beginning of the commercial thrust to tie electric trains to Christmas, and with good reason, because that is when competition between Lionel and American Flyer was really hot. In that decade, both companies spent tremendous amounts of money, primarily in December, on newspaper and magazine advertising across the country.

As early as 1917, Lionel had promoted its top-of-the-line trains as "just what you want for Christmas." The featured items were expensive, so connecting them with the traditional season of generous gifts seemed natural. Actually, the first Lionel catalog advertising, dated 1902, indicated that the new battery-operated trolley car would make a good "window display or holiday gift." Interestingly enough, this was before Lionel conceived of its products as children's toys—they were still being sold primarily as attention-getting animations for store windows. So, while the 1930s may have represented a watershed of sorts and signaled the start of intense seasonal advertising efforts, the bond between toy trains and Christmas was not really new.

The ad campaigns continued full blast through the 1940s, in spite of the fact that no new trains were produced during World War II, and reached their zenith in the 1950s, the acknowledged "Golden Age" of toy trains. By that time, television had also entered the media mix. Both Lionel and American Flyer sponsored pre-Christmas TV programs each year, highlighting their new product lines within a context of stories about real railroad adventures.

Interspersed amid these tales of high-iron heroism, the themes of family values and togetherness came through loud and clear in the advertising of the 1950s. The horrors of World War II, the cruelty of the Korean War, and anxiety over The Bomb all worked to pull families closer together and to return to "traditional" values. Building a layout to showcase the family's toy trains could provide a permanent bond between parents and children, because it was an activity in which everyone could participate. Toy trains were portrayed as a major focal point in the Great American Dream—tangible evidence of the abundance for all to be enjoyed in the tranquil and rosy Postwar Era.

But then a deluge of new high-tech toys—space rockets, robots, and computer games—diverted trains into a siding for about fifteen years during the 1960s and '70s. The advertising-driven popularity of different toys did not signal an end to toy trains, however; merely a transition—a shift in emphasis from children to a new generation of adult collectors and operators.

The toy train renaissance of the 1980s ultimately led to the development of better and more technologically up-to-date model trains, capable of satisfying more demanding adult tastes and requirements. Along with this came a resurgence of interest in creating holiday train displays. For the most part, these layouts are more thoughtfully conceived, carefully constructed, tastefully appointed, and elaborate than the old child-centered ones.

The most wonderful Christmas in any Boy's Life

...the day you give ...the day he gets

LIONEL TRAINS

This Lionel ad in a 1950s issue of *Boy's Life* magazine made the relationship between Christmas and toy trains crystal clear: "The most wonderful Christmas in any Boy's Life . . . the day you give . . . the day he gets Lionel Trains."

So, for many of us, toy trains under the tree have become integral to the way we celebrate Christmas—every bit as traditional as twinkle lights, ornaments, and evergreen garland. The difference, however, is that along with toy trains come cherished memories of play and of "quality time" spent with a parent, usually Dad. Those of us fortunate enough to have received toy trains for Christmas decades ago have steam engines and cabooses forever linked—coupled—to this happiest time of the year.

How far back does the toy train and Christmas connection go? Reverend Walter Plock treasures this charming photo of his father in front of the family Christmas tree. The train in the foreground is an American Flyer clockwork (windup) set. The photo was taken about 1910.

(Below.) Dewey Rice's family put together this classic standard gauge (with a smaller O gauge loop inside) Lionel layout in Washington, D.C., in the early 1930s. Because the train belonged to his older brother, five-year-old Dewey wasn't allowed to touch it. Today, however, through his long-time membership in the Train Collectors Association, Dewey has managed to locate examples of the same cars and locomotive. Now he can touch them as often as he wants to!

This warm photo of Michael and Lynda Boie's family room decorated for Christmas has trains in it every-where. A modern large scale train by German manu-facturer LGB circles the tree, and there are Lionel and MTH standard and O gauge models displayed on shelves and in cases around the room.

All the elements are here: Christmas tree, toy trains beneath it, fireplace, snowy morning, Dad, and . . . little brother. Oh well, nothing's perfect. Artist Angela Trotta Thomas (see page 44) pushes all the right buttons for kids who grew up in the 1940s, '50s, and '60s. Those familiar orange-and-blue Lionel cartons, Lionel tissue that protected the shiny paint on the cars and locomotives, and the corrugated cartons bearing the words "Lionel Trains" guaranteed that *this* would be a memorable Christmas!

(Top right.) Twelve-year-old Jim Owsinski is shown with his 1954 Christmas layout. Now sixty, Jim is still collecting and playing with trains, though he says, "I can't sit on the floor as I did in the photo!"

Richard Triano of Hillside, New Jersey, proudly holds the Lionel Santa Fe diesel that pulled his first train set on Christmas morning in 1957. Little did he know that the city he lived in would be familiar to young Lionel railroaders all over America. Hillside is a city not far from the Lionel factory, and that name is stamped onto the side of thousands of Lionel passenger cars sold in the 1950s. That meant nothing to Richard, though; all he cared about was that he got a train for Christmas. Note the nativity scene over Richard's shoulder—a wonderfully appropriate anachronism next to streamlined diesels and smoking steam locomotives.

Jim and Debby Flynn have an almost thirty-year tradition of Christmas toy train displays, beginning with a simple circle around the tree and culminating in what is shown here. A tasteful combination of regular train accessories and Department 56 buildings turns the three-level layout into a winter wonderland. It takes them well over a month to get set up each year.

The Flynns are almost single-handedly responsible for keeping the tradition of all-metal, tinplate trains alive in America. Since the early 1990s, when they acquired the rights and tooling, they have been manufacturing new Marx trains in the classic way, using

If the trains you want are no longer available, why not make your own? That's what Jim and Debby Flynn did. They were fans of the old Marx line and when tooling and rights became available, Jim and Debby decided to put the line back in production. The trains on their Christmas layout are all of their own manufacture.

sheet steel and colorful lithography. All of the trains appearing on their Christmas layout are of their own design and production.

Together, they planned and built a 6 by 11 movable layout in sections that fit together like a jigsaw puzzle. It has multiple levels, mountains, canyons, and road-ways. They constructed it in the basement and then moved it to the family room in time for Christmas.

The layout was originally intended to be in place for a single holiday season, but it remained for two. In the fourteen months it was on display, more than 200 friends and visitors viewed the layout.

New Marx trains wend their way through snowbanks
and pine trees as ice skaters enjoy the outdoors. The
buildings on the Flynns' layout are modern ceramic
structures, the figures are mostly vintage cast metal,
but the trains are all new Marx. What a great display
to show to friends and customers!

In this wonderful hand-tinted photo from the mid-1930s, Richard and Kenneth Funk stand tall next to their standard gauge display. Their mother, who was out when the photographer arrived, was horrified to see that the boys had put on coats and ties, but hadn't changed out of their "everyday" knickers—the ones with the worn spots on the knees. They were probably more interested in the trains than in sartorial matters.

Every Christmas as he was growing up, James Kempthorn had an extensive layout under his tree. The model church, at the upper left of this 1953 photo, contained an electric organ motor that flooded the scene with appropriate music. James says it "played a truly magical tune that I can still hear in my head to this day."

Colin Bennett gets some hands-on experience with toy trains while learning about the things that put food on his high chair. Colin is the son of *Classic Toy Trains* magazine advertising sales manager Dean Bennett. The odds are pretty good that Colin will grow up knowing the fun of toy trains around the Christmas tree.

The deep economic depression of the early 1930s was particularly hard on the American toy industry. People had little money to spend for non-essentials, even at Christmastime. Lionel's electric trains, quality products all, were considerably upscale and priced beyond the means of many in those dark days. Already in receivership, the company teetered on the brink of bankruptcy.

In a bold move late in 1934, Lionel decided to produce a line of animated windup handcars to retail at $1.00. This marked the company's first venture into the low end of the toy market, which was then dominated by Louis Marx and dozens of offshore manufacturers.

To differentiate its products from the mass of flimsy, nondescript Japanese playthings piled high on dime-store counters, Lionel entered into a licensing agreement with Walt Disney—possibly the first such arrangement in history—to use popular Disney characters on the handcars.

Mickey and Minnie Mouse appeared pumping the first one, which hit the stores before Christmas and sold out immediately. This success spawned a Santa Claus car, with Mickey peeking out of his backpack, as well as a Donald Duck and Pluto vehicle the next year.

A fourth car, featuring Peter Rabbit and a basket of Easter eggs, didn't fare as well. Perhaps, in the springtime, even very young men's fancies turn elsewhere.

Some historians credit the production of these charming handcars with turning the corner for Lionel and getting the firm out of receivership. While that might be a fanciful stretch, they certainly contributed toward rebuilding corporate health and paving the way to Lionel's most productive and profitable years, which were just ahead.

The family of Mark Schmotzer of St. Louis has cele-
brated Christmas with American Flyer trains around
the tree for half a century. Mark's father started the
tradition, and now his own children and grandchildren are enjoying it. The black-and-white photo
is from the early 1950s; the color photo is from the
late 1990s.

Both hands and intense concentration were needed if you wanted to be the engineer on a crack American Flyer passenger train. Ed Montgomery measured up to the task on Christmas morning of 1957. Two years later, Ed's sister Janet waited to join in the fun. According to Ed, Janet was interested in the trains as much as he was, though she was only five. "She even got her chance to run them."

Rick Evans was seven years old in 1962 when he got the American Flyer trains and Plasticville buildings that surround him. However, by the early 1970s all of the toys were packed up and forgotten—until 1996, when his year-and-half-old daughter got excited about the trains running under the Christmas tree at a relative's house. Now the same trains that are in the photo, and a few more, ride again at the Evans home each Christmas.

Greetings

1942

From The Websters

(Left.) One thing you could count on with Marx trains was colorful lithography, a process for printing on metal. The "Girard" station is one example. Another feature that Marx had that none of the other manufacturers used was backlit full-color inserts for the passenger car windows. Other manufacturers used a translucent glazing or featured black silhouettes of passengers. Jim and Debby Flynn put together this diorama featuring 1950s-vintage Marx trains for use as a Christmas card.

In the 1940s and '50s personalized Christmas cards were all the rage. This one from 1942 made use of special effects. Dick Webster is the little guy seated with his family on the "cowcatcher" of a Lionel standard gauge toy locomotive. He recalls that in his family steam engines were called "Chuggers."

Eleven-year-old Peter Siciliano and his father dispatch the train on their 1957 Christmas layout. Peter's uncle had to build the display because Mr. Siciliano worked sixteen-hour days in the family grocery store and couldn't find the time. With his loosened tie, he has the tired look of a man who works hard to support his family.

"Tru-Vue" was a stereoscopic filmstrip viewing system marketed in the 1930s. While not really sold as toys, the viewers were popular with children in those pre-television days, so a certain percentage of the filmstrips had themes of interest to youngsters. The photos from this particular one, called "Santa's Workshop," were shot on a Sunday at the old Chicago American Flyer factory in the summer of 1933. They clearly show the company's toy train production and testing facilities. The name of the man in the baggy Santa suit has been lost to history, but the boys dressed in gnome costumes were Robert and Kermit Cuff, sons of one of American Flyer's vice-presidents.

It's not clear whether Santa's North Pole toy shop made American Flyer trains or that Santa's elves worked nights at the American Flyer plant in Chicago! Whichever the case, the trains made lots of boys (note that sister has a doll) happy.

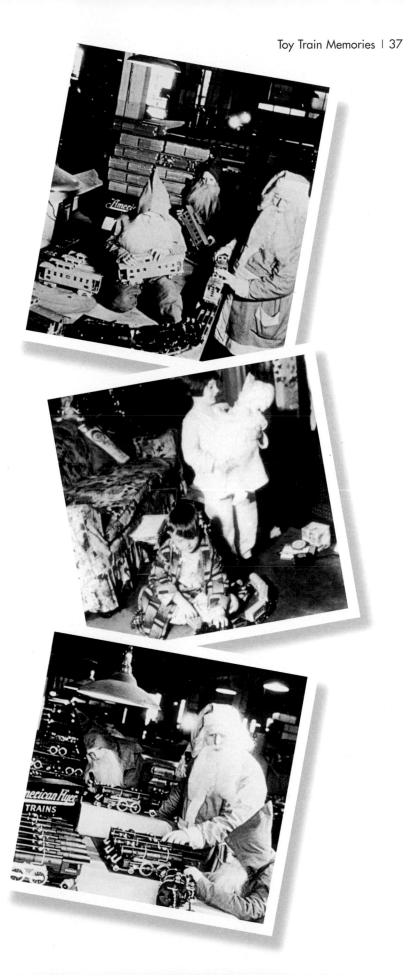

Creating the Dream
CATALOGS AND WISHBOOKS

In the fall of every year, Lionel and American Flyer toy train companies published large, full-color catalogs, to be distributed free at retail outlets or sent directly to customers for a small postage and handling fee. It was said that Lionel had a million of them printed and still ran short some years.

Fathers and sons spending time together—that's what Lionel and American Flyer ads promised. In fact, the annual train catalog represented the beginning of many lifelong father-son partnerships. Seven-year-old Robert Clark, of Etobicoke, Ontario, found a willing father to peruse the 1960 Lionel catalog with him.

These were major wishbooks in the hands of kids who pored over them until the pages were tattered and dog-eared. The artwork was larger than life, showing all of the new trains stretched out across the pages at eyeball level. Page after page featured colorful arrays of accessories in action: coal, lumber, and cattle being loaded on a siding; baggage-cart drivers whizzing in and out of the freight station; *The Limited*, smoke billowing from her stack, whistle shrieking, and lights blinking, as she races past a blue-uniformed gateman on her way to Lionelville.

The catalog copy far outstripped the word "puffery" in vivid description and explicit detail. It tweaked the imagination glands, inspired dreams, and instilled something akin to green-eyed lust in the hearts and minds of young readers. How could any child possibly survive without these incredible new toys under the Christmas tree?

The train catalogs served an important disciplinary and behavior-adjustment function as well. From the time the catalogs

appeared—usually between Halloween and Thanksgiving—rooms were kept clean, beds were made, toys put away, homework finished, teeth brushed, and ears washed, all without prompting or back-talk. Next to the patter of little feet dutifully marching off to bed on time, the only sounds parents were likely to hear were the thud of hints dropping. The curative effect train catalogs had on juvenile delinquency was amazing. It totally vanished—at least for a month or two.

Yet, interestingly enough, the train catalogs never made references to the holidays. There weren't even any winter scenes in them. Trains were shown by themselves or in real-railroad settings. Nevertheless, all of the advertising, point-of-purchase displays, factory production, and distribution were tightly focused on getting the line out and into the stores in time for Christmas. Why? The trains were marketed as Christmas gifts. But they weren't intended to have a limited seasonal appeal; they could be enjoyed—and sold—all year long.

What budding engineer could resist the appeal of the brilliant crimson-and-white *Texas Special* racing across the plains with a load of freight destined to keep the wheels of commerce rolling? Lionel printed millions of catalogs like this over the years; children wore them out as fast as Lionel could produce them.

Toy wholesalers, distributors, retailers, and mail-order companies were a different matter. Most of them published their own special Christmas catalogs and flyers showing toys and trains in traditional holiday settings, complete with the North Pole, Santa, the sleigh, the eight tiny reindeer, mistletoe, holly, the whole twelve yards.

Today, toy marketing is more sophisticated and more expensive. For Lionel and American Flyer, attractive forty-page color brochures were more than enough to generate excitement—and sales!

The 1952 Lionel catalog featured both steam and diesel locomotives, though steam was on its way out on the real railroads. The Santa Fe F unit, Lionel's best seller, was featured prominently at the left corner.

Often, toy train catalogs featured happy boys along with larger-than-life images of the toy trains themselves. Lionel artists were masters at creating dramatic views of speeding toy trains guaranteed to quicken the pulse. While the trains were always the focal point, the boy was never too far away. Massive electric and steam locomotives appear to race directly at us on this 1929 Lionel catalog cover, while the rosy-cheeked lad hovers over them, exulting in the knowledge that he controls these powerful brutes.

Joe Adda's father was an independent commercial photographer who did catalog work for Lionel in New York City. In fact, Joe posed for many shots, one of which was the basis for the cover of the 1929 Lionel catalog, shown above. The photograph (at left) of Joe and his first train was shot in 1928.

Angela Trotta Thomas, whose paintings appear elsewhere in this book, is the premier toy train artist of our day. Her paintings evoke nostalgic reminiscences of Christmases past—most of them relating to toy trains. Thomas, whose husband Bob is a toy train collector, became interested in the subject while researching Lionel catalog art for her master's thesis. She started out with trains and kids as her subject matter, and ended up launching a very successful career.

Most toy train enthusiasts have layouts in basements or garages. This layout is in the home of toy train artist Angela Trotta Thomas and husband Bob. Every layout is different, but this one is truly distinctive. The Thomases chose to make their basement layout represent a 1950s hobby shop. Note the kids looking in the window and door and the words in the window painted in reverse. In fact, window and door are paintings designed to make it look as though children are peering into the store. The effect is creative and very convincing.

The stunning Thomas family layout is more theme-oriented than most. Angela and her husband Bob have created the inside of a toy train store, down to the minutest detail, as it might have appeared at Christmastime in the 1950s. A mural painting of children peering into the window to see the trains clinches the illusion.

The train layout itself represents the store's operating display and combines her collection of illuminated Snow Village buildings with her husband's train and accessory collection. How's that for family unity?

Angela expressed it all this way: "The holiday season used to be intertwined with toy trains, so I wanted to have Christmas 365 days a year—something to showcase the trains and set a mood of holiday happiness."

Artist Angela Trotta Thomas's store window painting sets the scene of a 1950s train store, but the layout completes the illusion. Snow Village structures, die-cast vehicles, lots of lights, and trains in motion make for a great display. Because she has so wonderfully captured the essence and joy of toy trains, Lionel recently commissioned Angela to do a catalog cover for them.

Today's dads find it difficult to set aside enough time to build relationships with their children. Maybe it's always been that way. Maybe that's why, in the middle of the past century, Lionel and American Flyer ads stressed that toy trains could bring dads and sons together. After all, trains were "manly" things—big, powerful, fast, complex, working machines. It seemed natural that sons should be prepared for life in that world, and that was Dad's job. In fact, it did work that way for many boys. Many have fond memories of building layouts together, learning about electricity, learning how to fix a broken coupler. Perhaps dads didn't know it then, but they really were preparing their sons for life and work. Of course, as a side benefit, they got to play with the trains, too.

Jim Abbott and his dad began a father-son partnership based on toy trains at Christmas 1952. Like so many wonderful family traditions, it started small. James says, "I think my dad was having as much fun with it as I was!" Imagine that.

What do the stars in the background of Angela Trotta Thomas's painting represent? Dreams, aspirations? If that's the case, Dad is clearly sharing in them. The artist has captured the sense of joy and wonder toy trains represented to youngsters. She has also recognized how toy trains were a medium through which fathers and sons could communicate with and learn from each other. Lifelong father-son relationships began with toy trains.

In the early 1950s, a handful of Lionel employees traveled to Rochester, New York. Their assignment was to build a Lionel layout for the Police Athletic League (PAL), a charitable organization designed to bring together the city's youth and local police. The layout, divided into four scenes, one for each season, still exists and is being maintained by a group of local model railroaders. The scene pictured here represents winter; if you look closely, you can see Santa and his sleigh in the upper left corner.

Christmas 1940 in Lancaster, Ohio. On the carpet, ten-year-old David Donkle and his sister Betsey. David poses his new American Flyer train while Betsey reads aloud. At Betsey's elbow, a "modernistic" doll house. The Great Depression had made things rough for the Donkles, but David's dad had become an officer in the U.S. Army and was finally getting a regular paycheck. The kids shared in the newfound prosperity.

Four-year-old Robert Clark of Etobicoke, Ontario, with his first Marx windup train in 1957. In 1960 Robert got his first electric train. By then Lionel was cheapening its line as sales were declining. The set he got had no switches to provide operating variety, and the locomotive would run in one direction only. It was many years later, when his own son was born, that Robert took out the trains (having bought some switches) and started having fun with them. Today he regards himself as a toy train collector. "I have the trains displayed in a large curio cabinet in our family room, and they are a joy to look at. Indeed, I never tire of marvelling at the color and quality of these toys which were built fifty years ago."

In the late 1930s the Atchison, Topeka & Santa Fe railroad, whose routes traversed the desert Southwest, unveiled its newest diesel locomotives in what came to be known as the "warbonnet" scheme. The locomotive's bright red nose, accented with sweeping yellow stripes outlined in black, and the silver body were eye-catching and glamorous, somehow appropriate for the newly developing West Coast, Los Angeles, and Hollywood. Newsreels regularly featured movie stars boarding the *Super Chief* on their way to appearances in Chicago or New York. Because it was in the public eye, this flashy new paint scheme was a natural choice when Lionel decided to introduce its new F3

locomotive in 1948. The other paint scheme they chose was also a natural: the more sophisticated, blue-blooded eastern railroad—the New York Central in its classic pinstriped two-tone gray.

But it was the eye-catching red Santa Fe warbonnet that captured the toy train buyers' imagination in 1948 and into the 1950s. This colorful engine became a generic symbol that defined the toy train in America. Towing a string of warmly lighted aluminum passenger cars that shimmered with the reflected glow of red and green tree lights while moving among the gaily wrapped presents, this train, more than any other, spelled "Christmas" for generations.

Lionel's Santa Fe F3: the quintessential Christmas train. First offered in 1948, this locomotive has been a favorite in Lionel's toy train line for more than fifty years. It's the toy train Christmas classic, popular enough that Hallmark made it one of the first in its series of collectible toy train ornaments.

When one toy train company had success with a new product, the others quickly followed suit with versions of their own. First Lionel introduced the Santa Fe warbonnet F3 (top), followed by American Flyer's warbonnet version of another popular locomotive, the American Locomotive Company's beautiful PA. Not to miss out on a good thing, Louis Marx and Co. produced a lithographed tinplate version of the Santa Fe F3 (bottom). The striking warbonnet scheme—whether on a real locomotive or on a toy— is arguably the most recognized locomotive paint scheme of all .

Appearing in the Lionel catalog every year from 1948 to 1966, reissued in the late 1970s and twice during the 1990s, Lionel's O gauge model of Electro-Motive Corporation's double-unit Santa Fe diesel is the most popular toy train locomotive of all time, with sales topping the million mark.

Of course, Lionel's competitors paid attention and followed suit. Gilbert American Flyer came up with an S gauge replica of a different locomotive but with the same color scheme in 1950. A year later, Louis Marx produced an economy version in attractively lithographed sheet metal. It too sold very well.

And this timeless classic is still with us. In recent years, contemporary train makers, Lionel, K-Line, MTH, and Williams, have all offered their own interpretations of it. And that's not even considering all the models made from Z scale to G scale! The streamlined Santa Fe F3 diesel is truly the quintessential Christmas locomotive.

This Christmas morning picture of Kenneth Couch shows that sailor suits were very big in 1945, even among fledgling engineers. Don't let the pout fool you; Kenneth recalls that he was "thrilled to get [his] wish from Santa."

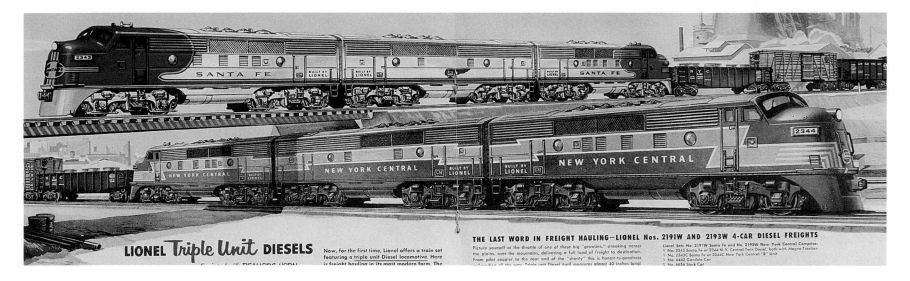

LIONEL Triple Unit DIESELS

Now, for the first time, Lionel offers a train set featuring a triple unit Diesel locomotive. Here is freight hauling in its most modern form. The

THE LAST WORD IN FREIGHT HAULING—LIONEL Nos. 2191W AND 2193W 4-CAR DIESEL FREIGHTS

Picture yourself at the throttle of one of these big "growlers," streaking across the plains, over the mountains, delivering a full load of freight to destination. From pilot coupler to the rear end of the "shanty" this is honest-to-goodness railroading all the way. Triple unit Diesel itself measures almost 40 inches long!

Lionel Sets No. 2191W Santa Fe and No. 2193W New York Central Comprise:
1 No. 2343 Santa Fe or 2344 N.Y. Central Twin Diesel, both with Magne-Traction
1 No. 2343C Santa Fe or 2344C New York Central "B" Unit
1 No. 6462 Gondola Car
1 No. 6656 Stock Car

To many who grew up during the 1940s and '50s, the accompanying artwork should seem familiar. Lionel catalog artist Robert Sherman did the line work for most of the catalogs during those decades, including the catalog pages above. His ability to make toy trains look real, while retaining their essential "toy-ness," bordered on genius. Whether his subject was a steam locomotive "hi-balling" freight across the prairie or a crack streamlined passenger train racing toward Lionelville, Bob made toy trains seem real. His style of commercial art resulted in the sale of Lionel trains by the hundreds of thousands. His role in the tremendous popularity of Lionel trains during mid-century can hardly be overstated.

Retired Lionel catalog artist Robert Sherman painted the Santa Fe F3 at left for *Classic Toy Trains* magazine. The low-angle view, which emphasizes the size, power, and speed of the streamlined locomotive, is characteristic of the artwork he created for Lionel's catalogs during the 1940s and '50s.

Carl Johnson (far left) didn't get the new trumpet for Christmas in 1952; that belonged to his brother, Lester. Carl had gotten a clarinet the year before. But the Johnson brothers, of Quincy, Illinois, both got toy trains. In fact, the fun of electric trains is a three-generation tradition in the Johnson family. The boys' father, Clyde, was a toy train enthusiast; then Lester and Carl got started in the hobby with their first trains in 1949; and now Carl's son, Kent, is a toy train enthusiast, columnist for *Classic Toy Trains* magazine, and railroad book editor. Carl and Kent attend flea markets together and work on each others' layouts.

Reminiscent of the story about the zoo animals who thought the bars on their cages were there to protect them from the people, four-year-old Ralph Albanese's train and Christmas tree were both located inside a playpen to keep them safe from one-year-old brother Sammy. Dated New York, 1950. Judging from the grin on Ralph's face, he thinks it's pretty funny too!

Charmingly toylike in every respect: trains, buildings, figures, and vehicles. Toy and train collector Gary Linden creates a whimsical Christmas display every year. His primary interest is in the toys manufactured by Louis Marx and Co., so he has lots of toys to choose from when he builds his holiday display.

Anthony Lamb treasures this photo (above) of his tinsel-covered tree and toy train layout from 1938, when he was four. His freight train was a Lionel, and the layout featured classic accessories: crossing gate, gateman, and coal loader. Remote-controlled accessories were popular and, though a little crude by today's toy train standards, must have seemed wondrous to children and adults alike. After all, electricity still wasn't in every home.

This scene on George Lindgren's Christmas tree layout was designed to capture the spirit and feel of Bedford Falls at Christmastime. Look closely with your imagination, and you might see Jimmy Stewart running through the streets.

In the 1950s and '60s every toy train layout featured Plasticville buildings. In fact, that's a Plasticville station in the center foreground of this photo. Nowadays, Department 56 and other ceramic structures (most of the buildings on this layout) are the buildings of choice on Christmas-tree layouts. This beautiful display was built by Robert Diller of North Plainfield, New Jersey, who built elaborate train displays with his father each year during the 1950s and '60s. He's recently revived the tradition with his daughter Teresa.

Chuck Bair with his train in 1961. One of the sets under the tree belonged to his father. Now Chuck shares all of them with his own son. Trains are like that—they bridge the generation gap in a way that few things can.

W. B. Mackensen is keeping a close watch on his Hafner windup train as it races around its loop of track in 1938. The photo captures the blur, so it's moving along pretty quickly. Being a windup model, the train goes slower and slower as the spring mechanism loosens. No chance to control its speed as with an electric train, but that's okay—W. B. is a little young to be playing with electricity. Many children started out with windup trains and graduated to electric.

Where Magic Happened
DEPARTMENT STORE WINDOWS

Every year from the day after Thanksgiving until Christmas, department

store windows all over the country were transformed into magical

domains, with dazzling, often animated holiday displays. While what

appeared there was dependent upon the budget and creativity of the

window dressing departments, it usually took the form of a fairy-tale,

fantasy-land portrayal of the secular story of Christmas. And, like the

circus and Disney theme parks, these wonderful panoramas were

designed to captivate children of all ages.

The cover of the 1949 Lionel catalog has it all: Santa Fe diesels, steam engines,
freight cars, passenger cars, accessories, and, most important, happy potential
customers. Lionel and American Flyer produced colorfully illustrated catalogs to
display their line and generate excitement about the trains. Then retailers followed
up by showcasing the trains in their own holiday window displays. No wonder the
young boy (in a suit and tie, no less!) with his hands pressed against the window is
so delighted; he's seeing the very trains pictured in his catalog in action!

Some of the more elaborate ones went over the top with life-size portrayals of the frenzied activities in Santa's North Pole workshop as the December 24th deadline approached. Elves tended machines with blinking lights, spinning wheels, bells, whistles, and spewing steam that turned out toys, candy canes, and Christmas trees. Other elves were busy loading the sleigh. All of this under the watchful supervision of old St. Nick himself; of course, there had to be electric trains somewhere in the scene.

Many of the larger stores had entire windows devoted exclusively to elaborate toy train layouts. Others displayed bountiful arrangements of all sorts of toys, with trains providing eye-catching movement as they wound their way among the other treasures.

A great example of this kind of window exhibit appears in the 1983 classic film, *A Christmas Story*. In the opening scene, behind the title and credits, we see four trains running around and through a mountain of toys in the corner window of a mythical department store in 1940s Indiana. Kids are standing earmuff to earmuff, with their noses pressed against the glass.

Major market retailers like Field's, Gimbel's, Macy's, and Neiman Marcus all had extravagantly decorated windows at Christmas, but even in the smaller cities department stores went all out. For example, Prange's department store in Sheboygan, Wisconsin, always featured both kinds of displays—the general Christmas scenes with Santa and his entourage, as well as windows

The Famous-Barr department store of St. Louis featured an entire window devoted to trains each Christmas season. The store tried to integrate the train layout with themes carried out in their other animated window scenes. One year, a touch control wired to the outside allowed onlookers to stop and start one of the trains. While not as realistic as the displays of the 1950s, the 1974 train window featured avant-garde sheets of colored Plexiglas in the shapes of mountains.

loaded with toys, featuring at least two Lionel trains running continuously, even after store hours. Apparently, the window dressing overhead was deemed worthwhile.

The golden era for these spectacular animated store window displays ran from the Great Depression years of the early 1930s, when many people were looking for something bright to lift their spirits, to the late 1950s. After that, the displays became less lavish. Fewer windows were devoted to Santa Claus. There were more static presentations of other holiday-related things—Christmas merchandise shown in family settings, home and hearth, food and drink, mistletoe and holly, even some Dickensenian scenes. Christmas was becoming more sophisticated.

Or was it? Maybe the shift in emphasis had to do with broader changes in merchandising, brought on by department store mergers amid the rise of discount outlets. Maybe it was all the bright, young MBAs in three-piece suits who had suddenly taken over the retail marketing field. For whatever reason, much of the warmth and child-like charm disappeared.

Fortunately, the memory of those elaborate, but straightforward, Christmas windows is clear in the minds of those who stood, transfixed, as they gazed at the season's new electric trains winding their way endlessly through the other less-prized toys of Christmas.

Thanksgiving is over and Christmas 1947 is approaching. A great American family tradition of the mid-twentieth century was to go downtown to visit Santa and see how the merchants had decorated their windows. The Bon Marché store in Seattle, Washington, had huge American Flyer layouts built in its store window. Scenes like this were by no means unique; crowds gathered before the windows of major department stores all over America as the countdown proceeded between Thanksgiving and Christmas.

The black-and-white photo at top was taken in the early 1950s. The American Flyer layout, a real crowd-pleaser, graced a corner window of Seattle's Bon Marché department store. The two accompanying color photos were taken in the mid-1990s when two Seattle toy train enthusiasts built a new version of the layout for the same department store window.

During the late 1940s and early '50s, the Bon Marché department store of Seattle devoted an entire window to a large, almost museum-quality display of Gilbert American Flyer trains. The creator of this magnificent slice of life, Bob James, used S gauge trains in the foreground and smaller HO trains in the mountains to provide a dramatic sense of perspective. Everything worked and looked right. Operating accessories were placed in settings that made them seem more realistic. Even the river barges floated on real water. It was a terrific crowd pleaser.

Then, in 1994, Scott McAbee, with the help of Bob James (the original builder), decided to re-create the display. Bon Marché management was enthusiastic about the project and agreed to prominently display the American Flyer layout in the store windows. Once again it drew crowds to the windows and, better yet, into the store.

Christmas Moments

You don't find many train layouts in department store windows these days, but this may be the next best thing. Shown here is the winter scene on a three-rail traveling layout built by Harry Turner. The layout was built in a trailer and traveled all over the country in the 1990s to promote Lionel (and more recently MTH) trains. Somehow the bright colors of the trains just seem to jump out of the white snow background. The train, the snow, the church, and the ski hill in the distance evoke memories of "the season."

There's a cliché that goes with toy trains and Christmas. Fathers say they're buying toy trains at Christmas for their sons, but in fact, they're buying them for themselves. The painting at left, by Angela Trotta Thomas, called "My turn yet, Dad?" is based on that cliché. There's truth to it, but Junior eventually got the trains when Dad found other things to do. Lucky was the child, however, whose father found time to play with the trains again.

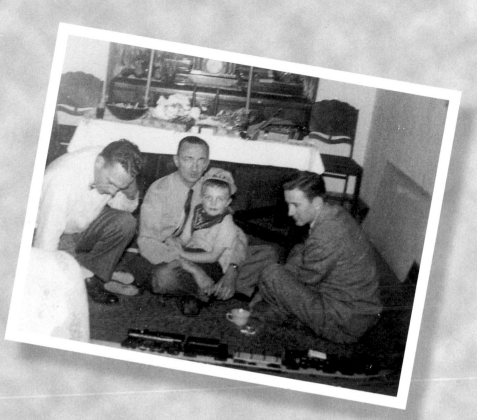

Whose train is this anyway? That's what Dick Christianson was probably thinking on Christmas Eve 1950. That's his dad at the controls to the left; uncle Jean is on the right; and uncle Irv is serving as a chair for Dick. Eventually the uncles went home, and Dick and his dad got to play with the trains together. In fact, over the years, they built at least three large layouts together. Lucky boy.

Scott T. Hanson has done some very creative and appealing things with his "Lionel City" station and terrace for his annual standard gauge holiday floor layout. Inspired by New York's Grand Central and Philadelphia's Thirtieth Street stations with their multi-level approaches, Hanson expanded the layout and made the Lionel station and terrace not only the centerpiece, but part of the tree stand as well.

With a piece of plywood under where the tree would be, he laid down some cement blocks and built a facade resembling the architecture of the model Lionel station. Next came four wooden passenger platforms and hardwood dowel support columns. Then he painted the new construction to match the colors of the original station.

The tree stand was placed directly behind the station, allowing the branches to drape over the roof and sides of it. The result was stunning, with trains running under the station and the tree as well, on a simulated underground level.

The tasteful decorating, the antique ornaments, and the vintage trains combine to paint a definitive scene of an elegant Christmas at the beginning of the twentieth century.

Railroad fan and toy train collector Ken Kelley deserves a special award for the most unusual supporting structure for his Christmas display. Kelley bought an old, dilapidated Railway Express Agency baggage cart at an auction and restored it to its original glory.

When the job was done, the cart seemed like a natural place for his holiday layout. On it, Ken arranged two loops of track on two levels and a delightful array of Lionel pre-World War II trains and accessories from his extensive collection.

There are many portable train layouts around, but very few truly mobile ones. Ken has wheeled his cart to train shows, schools, and even business offices. Young and old alike are enthralled by the antique trains, still chugging after almost three quarters of a century.

(Top right.) Two-and-a-half-year-old Robert Hendel learns to operate his new train in this 1938 photo, taken by his father on Christmas morning. Sectional tinplate track, such as the kind that came with Robert's train, was great for carpet-running and reassembly every holiday season. It was also oversized so that little hands could easily put the trains on the track. Robert still owns this original set.

One of the most wonderful things about toy trains is that they were so well built that they can be passed on from generation to generation. George Baker III, in the center of everything, inherited these trains from his grandfather and now runs them every Christmas for his own two sons. That's George's uncle, Joseph O'Keefe, connecting sections of track so the trains can roll!

Fred Severson tries to create a three-dimensional Christmas card with his layouts, emitting the peace, warmth, and charm of the season. His first train arrived when Fred was six or seven, and he's had a different Christmas layout every year since. This was the eighteenth one under his tree, more elaborate and detailed than most permanent layouts and just as operationally sophisticated. Fred is an electrical engineer and has installed many electronic "hands off" control devices.

On this particular layout, there are two towns, 1,000 miniature trees, 200 lights, many accessories, and special effects such as recorded Christmas carols coming from the church and an ice rink with moving skaters. A number of the automobiles have working headlights, and there are literally hundreds of little people in the streets.

The realistic snow is created from five different white materials, including cotton batting, Dacron batting, titanium dioxide powder, paint, and commercial spray snow.

The layout used to be a Thanksgiving-to-Christmas project. However, this extraordinary one was planned in July and construction began in September.

Fred Severson's "seasonal" layout is as impressive as any permanent toy train layout you're likely to see. Featuring sophisticated electronics, lighting, and animation, Severson's layout shows that he recognizes the connection between toy trains and Christmas—in a big way.

(Left.) A Christmas tree lot under a Christmas tree! Fred Severson has mini-scenes like this all over the layout. It must be difficult to come up with a different layout every year, but he's been doing it for years. Actually, that's part of the charm and genius of toy trains. You can put them together and take them apart in next to no time at all.

Passengers wait in the cold as "The General" rounds the curve and comes to a halt. It's an anachronism, but remember, these are toy trains, not scale models. Most toy train fans aren't fazed by inconsistencies. After all, the trains were built as toys.

(Above.) Passengers crowd the platform as the Southern Pacific *Daylight* pulls into town. Maybe it's Christmas Eve and the people are all anxious to get home to their families. Layout builder Fred Severson has hundreds of figures to put in place on his annual toy train layout under the tree. From year to year, it's never the same.

Reflected in the mirror-golden ornament, the little under-the-tree village seems to be filled with activity. Cars, trucks, and taxis work their way through snow-covered streets. Traffic lights control the intersections, and shoppers cross streets or wait at the curb. The village square has a tree decorated with lights and garland.

That tinplate shovel-nose locomotive with its Rudolph-red nose fits right into the toylike nature of this 4 by 8-foot layout built by the editorial staff of *Classic Toy Trains* magazine. Their intent was to evoke the spirit of Christmas layouts of the 1930s and '40s, using Department 56 buildings, cotton snow, lighted accessories, and vintage trains.

Classic Toy Trains, the premier magazine for people who love to collect and operate toy trains of all vintages and gauges, was established in 1987. Over the years, the editors and staff of the magazine have created a number of portable layouts to display the latest in toy train products and technology at train shows, meets, and fairs.

Among the most popular of these was the 1999 "North Pole" layout, which had a winter wonderland theme and combined the latest Department 56 ceramic buildings with contemporary plastic trackside accessories and pre-World War II-style sheet-metal trains. Somehow, it all seemed to fit together and look just right.

In the popular 4 by 8 size (standard sheet of plywood), the track plan forms a "wobbly hourglass" instead of the more-typical oval, because that allows the train to weave in and out of the city scene, disappearing and reappearing as it goes along.

The Department 56 illuminated ceramic buildings, and the self-actuating accessories—crossing gates, warning lights, and the like—are all readily available new products. However, the trains shown are all-metal Lionel antiques from the 1930s, selected because their toylike appearance fits in well with the Christmas-past look of the layout.

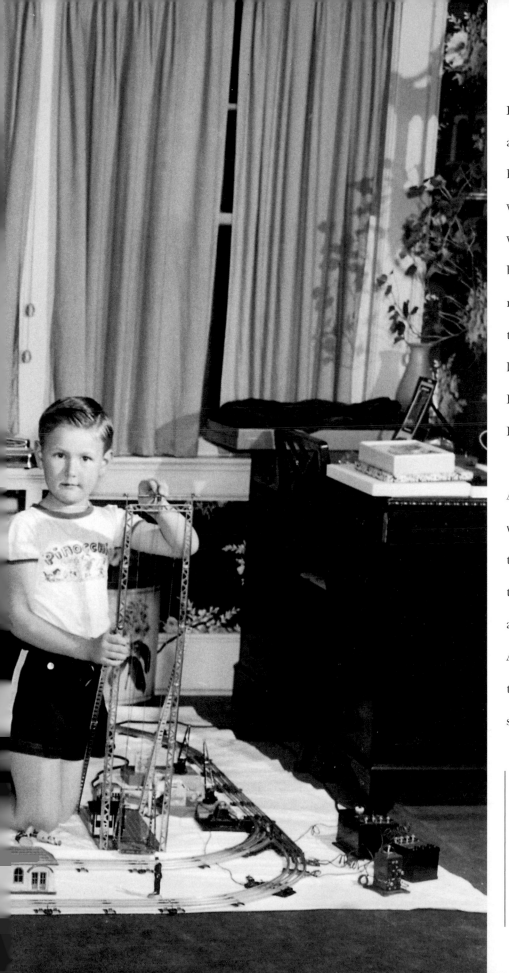

Presents weren't plentiful in many post-Depression and pre-World War II American homes. Those were hard times. But by 1940, some families had begun to work their way out of their financial difficulties and were able to offer their children gifts that would brighten their Christmas morning. The scene at left represents the way we prefer to remember those times. Christmas tree with lots of tinsel. Handsome little guy with slicked-down hair. A "Kewpie doll" sister. Lots of gifts, including stuffed animals, a doll, an Erector Set, and a Lionel toy train under the tree.

Reality, of course, was often different. Lionel and American Flyer trains were never "cheap" toys; they were very high quality with a price tag to match. At the time this photo was taken (late 1930s), a typical train set would have been a week's wages for the average American man. In most homes, a Lionel or American Flyer train on Christmas morning meant that children were loved a great deal—and that sacrifices were made elsewhere.

Christmas morning 1938 or 1939 in the Morley household. Looks like Kenneth (about six years old) and his sister Ann hit the mother lode when it comes to presents. Kenneth, who eventually became an M.D. and has since returned to the fun of toy trains in retirement, recognizes how lucky he was. "I was an extremely fortunate youngster during a time most of the world was in great turmoil."

FOUR

Catalogs Brought to Life
THE TOY DEPARTMENT

Retailers that sold electric trains were encouraged by American Flyer,

Lionel, and other manufacturers to have demonstration tracks set up so

customers could see the toys in action. Lionel was the most insistent about

this and at one time issued a pamphlet outlining procedures and making

suggestions on how to sell the trains most effectively. Attractive merchan-

dise displays and personal demonstrations were considered essential.

From this, the familiar point-of-sale, in-store display layouts evolved.

In 1953, a youngster named Mike Novak was photographed gazing intently at the
American Flyer train display in New York's F.A.O. Schwarz toy store. Lionel and
Flyer went to great lengths to set up displays in major department stores in an
effort to attract attention to their trains, especially around Thanksgiving. Clearly, at
least in the case of this American Flyer layout, the strategy worked.

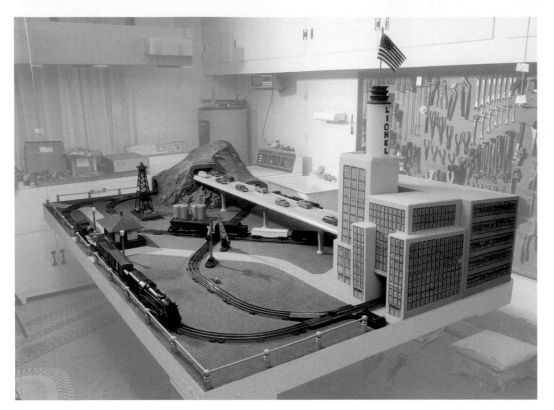

This remarkable Lionel display layout from 1952 was restored to its original luster by toy train enthusiast Darl McDaniel. With miniature automobiles moving along the highway and a magnificent skyscraper in the corner, this layout was more elaborate than the typical displays coming out of the Lionel factory. Once Lionel knew how many displays were sold to retailers for the upcoming season, the factory hired employees to turn them out assembly-line style.

Some stores were quite creative and turned these demonstration tracks into little slices of life, complete with tunnels, bridges, stations, and trackside accessories. Many had trains running continuously to attract attention.

At one time, Lionel actually had a department that did nothing but build displays and layouts for sale to dealers. The displays ranged in size from 4 x 6 to 8 x 8 and were available to retailers at attractive prices.

During the peak years in the 1950s, this department turned out as many as 3,000 units each year. In several designs and sizes, and with track plans that changed every year to accommodate the new line and to showcase accessories, these layouts—complete with scenery—were intended for small- and medium-sized retailers. The larger stores with more space built their own, often with the help of Lionel consultants.

The layouts served the dual purpose of showcasing the newest models released for the Christmas season and, more important, of attracting young customers—and their parents—into the toy department. All the trains around the Christmas trees in the photos in this book are testimony to how successful the manufacturers' efforts were.

The late Harry Osisek Jr., a collector of pre-World War II toy trains, had this marvelous display layout in his collection. The 3 x 5-foot O gauge layout, offered in 1922, originally sold for $100. Displays in such fine condition are mostly in the hands of collectors. The black-and-white photo is the catalog page on which the display was originally advertised.

Had you gone into a department store or hobby shop in the 1950s, you might have seen both of these displays, or ones like them. The large wall-hanging once graced the walls of a train shop, and the factory-built layout in the foreground was used to demonstrate all the latest Lionel offerings. Both of these are now owned by PGA Senior Tour golf professional Ed Dougherty. Ed's collecting specialty is Lionel displays.

Even in today's world of hi-tech electronics, video, and digital technology, children still find the sounds, colors, and motion of toy trains enthralling. This photo of Mike Novak was shot in the toy department of New York's F.A.O. Schwarz in 1953, but toy train layouts today draw the same rapt attention from youngsters.

The showroom at Lionel's New York City headquarters at one time included this mock-up of a typical toy department, complete with clerk and, not surprisingly, a display layout being scrutinized by a "customer."

Artist Angela Trotta Thomas has made toy trains her specialty. In this work, Thomas has captured the look of a typical department store display layout of the 1950s. Train manufacturers shipped layouts to the stores or traveled on location to build them in the store. The day after Thanksgiving the trains were up and running and attracting every child in the store to the toy department. Great times to be growing up!

Tony Magano (with sister and mom) of Wanaque, New Jersey, is running a very unusually mixed train, featuring a steam locomotive, passenger car representative of the 1960s, and another modeled after cars of the 1800s. But none of that matters to Tony on Christmas Day, 1962.

Now here's a happy little guy, and well he should be. It's 1959 and two-and-a-half-year-old Bob Wagner of Brooklyn, New York, has just received his first train set. He had no idea at the time, but he was embarking on a life-long hobby. Bob still has the trains shown in the photo and many, many more that he runs on a very large layout.

Broadway set designer Clark Dunham is a toy train enthusiast. When he's not building Tony-award-winning sets, he custom-builds layouts for clients. Clark built the layout shown here filling a large room in Doug DuBay's hobby shop in Des Moines, Iowa. Doug's extensive toy train collection was displayed, museum-like, in cases around the outside walls, but the enormous layout was the star of the show. It was a great attraction and attention-getter, and customers had the opportunity to see all the latest Lionel trains and accessories in action before they bought them.

The root of the word "decoration" is "décor." The Mark Edwards family decorates for Christmas in the root sense of the word. Move furniture to make room for toy trains in the seasonal decorating? Humbug! Run the track around and under it.

The Edwardses have been running trains on the floor at Christmas since Mark's great-grandfather started the tradition under the tree and behind the sofa in 1921. Mark has created a system of modules to expedite the project and to keep the carpeting clean.

The Mark Edwards family loves trains and Christmas. They love them so much that they make their American Flyer trains part of their seasonal decorating. In this family, under the tree simply isn't enough; under the table and behind the couch is standard operating procedure. The layout is amazingly elaborate for a temporary set-up.

The Edwardses have integrated the layout beautifully into their living area. Surprisingly, or perhaps not, the trains seem to belong. That in itself is strong evidence that Christmas and toy trains have become entirely natural partners.

Christmas Eve at Grand Central Station—miniature version, that is. This charming scene is lighted by the glow from windows and dome of the Marx passenger cars and streetlights. Jim and Debby Flynn build a home layout every year featuring Marx trains, noted for their tinplate construction and excellent lithographed detail.

(Clockwise from top.) Still not fully awake on Christmas Morning 1952, seven-year-old Donald Fletcher of Lehigh Acres, Florida, gets ready to operate his first electric train. Two years later, the trains are back around the tree, and Donald, first in pajamas and later in his railroad-engineer outfit, has more trains to be proud of: a stock car and handcar, and a coal hopper. Manufacturers had to love the progression: sell a train set the first year, then sell track, cars, locomotives, and accessories in subsequent years. Add-on sales at Christmas guaranteed!

The Grandinetti family, Mike and Mae and their daughters Michelle and Roseanne, all work on their annual Christmas project, which combines Department 56 collectible ceramic buildings and Lionel trains in a detailed, yet wonderfully uncluttered setting.

It is a seasonal display, designed to inspire peace and goodwill, which runs from Thanksgiving through New Year's Day each year and is based upon the Christmas layout Mike grew up with in the 1960s. He wants his daughters to experience the same magic he knew then.

Mike's father first built a 4 by 8 layout for the two trains he inherited from his uncle. He sandwiched it between the Christmas tree and the nativity set—the only available space. All aspects of Christmas were covered.

The Grandinetti family Christmas layout is now roughly 8 by 8, and one of Mike's original trains still runs on it. The lights and attention to detail make it work. The snow is simply Polyfil over white paint.

When one of Mike's friends saw the layout, he exclaimed, "This is Christmas! The only thing missing is Jimmy Stewart running down the street yelling, 'Merry Christmas, everybody.'"

Christmas is a time of giving and of sharing. Mike Grandinetti wanted to share the joy of his childhood Christmases with his wife and daughters by making toy trains a big part of their holiday celebration. So, each year they work together to build an 8 by 8-foot layout in their living room. It features toy trains and Department 56 ceramic buildings.

It's a race between steam and diesel on the Grandinetti's annual Christmas layout. There's magic in the the horns and whistles, the shiny paint, and the clatter of wheels clicking over track joints.

(Left.) Ken Chelosky operates his Lionel Scout train while "Sis" smiles at the camera in 1952. Two years later the Scout is on the siding and the crack streamlined Santa Fe Super Chief has taken its place. Now the layout board is painted green—left over from house painting last summer—and features Plasticville houses, a church, telephone poles, billboards, and a railroad station at Bethlehem. The Marx crossing gate is there to protect the Three Wise Men. Sis got a doll in 1954, the traditional Christmas gift for a girl in those days.

George Lindgren's Christmas tree train is popular with the grandchildren. The beaming smile, the intense concentration—priceless!

Step back to Christmas morning 1949 and look at what the Romagna brothers (John and Rob) found under their tree: two brand-new Marx windup trains, Lincoln Logs, a wooden "woodie," a book, some games, and a pressed-paper gas station. All in all, a nice Christmas.

Paul Wasserman has loved toy trains for years. His extensive collection of vintage train sets is second to none and includes some rare, one-of-a-kind items.

On his sweeping, multi-level, "waterwings-shaped" layout, Wasserman has practically every important operating and illuminated trackside accessory ever made. The panorama is breathtaking.

However, Paul has not forgotten how it all began for him and many other train collectors. In the center of the spread, there is an island with a permanent winter scene, complete with artificial snow and a little Christmas tree with a simple oval of track around it.

To toy train fans, the Christmas-toy train connection is as natural as breathing. So, when they build layouts, they often feature snow scenes. That's what toy train collector Paul Wasserman did. Trains line the walls of his display room, and in the center is a large operating layout. Part of that layout features snow and a Christmas tree—a nod of the head to the origins of his hobby.

FIVE

Toy Trains Sell
WORKING FOR COMMERCE AND CHARITY

For one hundred years now, the compelling nature of toy trains has been used to great advantage by a variety of businesses, particularly during the holiday season. Having a train running in a store window display, for example, attracts passers-by of all ages, inviting them to pause long enough to notice whatever other merchandise might be shown there. Often, that can be enough to get potential customers to enter the store. At the very least, it can make onlookers feel good about the place by getting them in a holiday mood. A positive in any case.

Central Ohio Chevrolet dealer Carl Nourse sets up an elaborate display of Lionel trains from his personal collection on his showroom floor every Christmas season. In an average year, 3,000 people come to the dealership to see the trains in action—many come with groups ranging from day care centers to nursing homes. All are drawn by the irresistible combination of trains and Christmas. Some even take a moment to look at the cars.

In a November 1953 *Saturday Evening Post* ad, Lionel development engineer Frank Pettit shared a good cup of coffee—notice the broad smile—with one of Lionel's model-makers in their "top-secret" lab in Irvington, New Jersey. In the photo to the right, we have Dad, son, coffee, and Lionel trains. You wonder who paid whom for the promotion!

Ronald McDonald and the Hamburglar aren't the only things that attract kids to McDonald's, in addition to the Happy Meals, of course. This franchise in Buena Park, California, included toy trains in its décor when the doors opened in 1989. The layout featured LGB trains (from the German toy company Lehmann) and was a real crowd-pleaser. So, did the kids come for the fries or to see the trains? Probably both.

Lionel's first electrically powered miniature railroad products were little gondola cars—without locomotive!—that ran around on a circle of track. They were intended to literally move merchandise by carting it around the inside of shop windows. Surprisingly, customers clamored to buy them as toys for their children. From that humble start in 1901, the one-time world's largest toy train company grew.

I can remember two instances from my youth where hometown businesses used toy trains to boost sales. Eagle Insulation, a company that treated older houses with their product to cut down on heating costs, had an American Flyer freight train running in its show window. All of the gondola cars were filled with Eagle's bulk insulation, and the boxcars had company decals on their sides. Of course, the model houses on the layout had Eagle trucks parked outside.

Even a small shoe store near my school had a train in the window. An upscale Lionel freight meandered through a winter landscape, amid shoes and shoeboxes wrapped in Christmas paper. All the kids stopped to watch it on the way home. Oh, how I wanted that train! None of us cared about the shoes.

Of course, toy trains, with their wholesome, all-American Christmas-morning image, have a halo effect. Over the years many products have associated themselves with toy trains: radios, soft drinks, cereal manufacturers. You can hardly watch television the month or two before Christmas without seeing a commercial that, however briefly, features a toy train circling a Christmas tree. Associating your product with toy trains is still good business.

Today, the tradition of setting up holiday train displays in places of business is very much alive. You'll find them in some of the most unlikely locations—banks, insurance companies, utilities, industrial offices, shopping malls, theaters, even clothing stores. Maybe the business owner is just a toy-train enthusiast indulging himself a little; but in most cases, business owners know that toy trains at Christmas generate traffic.

Norman Rockwell is famous for his paintings of American life. In December of 1950, one of his paintings graced a *Saturday Evening Post* ad for DuMont television sets. This one was prophetic in suggesting that children (and their black cocker spaniel!) would be captivated by television. If you look closely at the ignored Christmas presents on the floor behind the children, you'll see to the boy's right the end of a circle of three-rail Lionel track. Just above Rockwell's signature on the right is part of a Lionel Southern Pacific-style caboose—evidently one of this year's presents. Not only is Rockwell suggesting that television would capture the attention of American children, he was rightly predicting that even toy trains would fade into the background for the TV generation.

Trains can also be put to charitable uses. Years ago Lionel set up a layout in New York's Grand Central Station, and travelers could watch the trains run by contributing to the Fresh Air Fund, a charitable organization designed to get underprivileged children out of the city and to summer camp. More recently, The Galleria shopping mall in Dallas erected this seasonal layout, called "The Wonderland Express." First erected in 1988 and expanded each holiday season, the layout's trains ran continuously from Thanksgiving to New Year's. The attractive display, which emphasized adult memories and childhood fantasy, proved very successful—during peak hours, there was sometimes an hour-long wait to buy tickets. Proceeds went to the Easter Seal Society and the Ronald McDonald House.

The Cinergy Corporation (formerly Cincinnati Gas and Electric) has set up this gigantic O gauge model railroad display in their corporate headquarters every holiday season since 1946. Originally built by the B&O Railroad a decade before, this magnificent layout is open to the public. By Cinergy's count, 7.5 million visitors have enjoyed this Christmas tradition over the past fifty years.

Cincinnati's Cinergy layout (shown above in the 1950s) is a wonderland of lights and motion. As many as ten trains can run simultaneously on the layout. That takes a lot of power, but then, that's what Cinergy is all about.

Cinergy Corp. certainly recognizes the relationship between toy trains and Christmas. The beautiful display has graced its lobby for more than fifty years. It takes a strong commitment by the company to keep it going, but commitment also is given by the dozens of employees and former employees who maintain and repair the layout when it's not on display, and then run the trains and answer questions when it is on display during the holidays.

Lights, motion, color, sound. That's most of what it takes to captivate the hearts of children at Christmas. Toy trains provide all of that; simply add the seasonal decorations and you have a winning combination. When it comes to toy trains, it's easy for adults to become kids again, just for a while.

The GAP clothing store in Manhattan unveiled a large, snow-covered layout of Lionel trains during the 1995 holiday season. The store manager said the operating display highlighting GAP products evoked a sense of fun that reflected the store's youthful spirit. Cars were custom-decorated with GAP logos, and freight cars carried GAP products (albeit small ones). The layout in a department store should ring all kinds of nostalgia bells for Baby Boomers.

This 10 by 16-foot toy train layout was displayed in
the GAP store in downtown Manhattan in 1995.
Featuring custom-painted GAP cars and locomotives
and promoting GAP products, the layout was built
off-site in sections over a six-week period.

Five-year-old Rod Henshaw didn't have a chance. Railroading was in his blood. He was born in Altoona, Pennsylvania, site of the Pennsylvania Railroad's huge shop complex. Both of his grandfathers worked for the Pennsy there. What's especially interesting about this photo, taken on Christmas Day 1956, is the train beneath the tree. It's an HO scale Varney model of the real Aerotrain that Rod and his mother had ridden from Harrisburg to Altoona and back earlier the same year. "Truth be told," says Rod, "that Varney engine never really ran very well, but we still have it, and it forms part of the tapestry of Christmas memories that our family has woven around toy trains." The old Aerotrain has been retired, but it still serves as a memory of one of the best Christmas gifts a five-year-old ever received.

One of Broadway set designer Clark Dunham's custom-built layouts, called "America on Parade," is an attraction in a shopping area of Williamsburg, Virginia. Clark builds layouts when he's not building sets. The Broadway influence is big on his layouts, which feature discrete scenes and scenery flats. His layouts are visually stunning and entertaining to view. In the closeup at right, a Southern Pacific F unit pulls into a station somewhere in the Sierra Mountains.

New York's famous Hell Gate Bridge is the star of this scene, built by Broadway set designer Clark Dunham. The layout was built for a display in Williamsburg, Virginia, called "America on Parade." Christmas wreaths, ice skaters, skiers, a sleigh—even if it's hot and muggy in Virginia, it's always Christmas on this layout. Dunham put lots of those very popular ceramic buildings to good use. The glow of light coming through their windows adds signs of life and warmth to this cold winter scene.

Most of the trains featured in this book are manufactured in the United States. The one in these two photos, however, was made in Germany. Michael Noday served in Europe during World War II and brought the Märklin electric train home to Youngstown, Ohio, at war's end. That's Michael's wife Mary in the first photo, taken in 1950. When Mike Jr. was born in 1952, the train was ready and waiting for him. The Noday family believed in advance planning.

In the 1950s, when toy trains were at their peak as the toy of choice, train displays were featured in department stores everywhere. Shopping malls were largely a thing of the future, and few could have imagined how toy trains could someday be used to enhance Christmas decorations in those large venues. The Albany (Georgia) Mall center court display is a modern example of how that works. The 17-foot-high, four-sided exhibit, depicting traditional holiday scenes (Musicland, Candyland, Toyland, and the Nutcracker Suite), featured fifteen trains running simultaneously. The exhibit was maintained by a local model railroad club.

A pedal car *and* trains—what a lucky little guy! The display under the tree, with its house and picket fence, is elaborate, but not extraordinarily so. In many homes, the "Christmas village" was as traditional as the tree itself and families went to great lengths to make it special. In this case, there was no train. Maybe the windup in the foreground ended up under the tree the following year.

(Below.) In the 1960s and later, "Some assembly required" became a phrase dads dreaded to read on Christmas Eve. That innocent word "some" invariably translated into hours of difficult work and frustration. From the look of frustration on Stan Williams' face, he seems to be having some difficulty with the Lionel under the family tree in 1972. Lionel trains were actually built to be dad-friendly. Snap the tracks together, attach two wires, put the train on the track, and watch it run.

Perhaps the ultimate toy train and Christmas connection: trains themselves decorated for the holiday. These fanciful pieces—a steam engine, a Santa handcar, and a caboose—were all made by LGB, a German toy train manufacturer. For many years Lionel offered specially painted Christmas boxcars; customers could have trains of nothing but brightly colored Christmas boxcars circling their tree. Toy trains promoting the toy train-Christmas connection. Novel idea!

The Huntington National Bank of Columbus, Ohio, whose sister city is Dresden, Germany, builds a gigantic lobby display each year, featuring large-scale, European-style trains amid a model German village. The bank considers the layout to be a community service—a tool to reach families and school groups in the area, and to give something back to their customers. The 600-square-foot display draws as many as 6,000 people in an evening during the holiday season.

SIX

Movies and Television Made the Connection
CELEBRITIES AND TOY TRAINS

Toy trains have been used in motion pictures numerous times over the years, either as part of the plot or as attractive backgrounds and set dressings. Three Christmas-themed film classics in which toy trains appear come to mind immediately: *A Christmas Story, A Holiday Affair,* and *Miracle on 34th Street.*

Early television also found toy trains appealing. Of course, almost anything that provided interesting motion for the small black-and-white screens was welcomed. Lionel executives and sales reps had appeared on local New York and Chicago shows to demonstrate their new products as early as 1947, with good apparent response.

A young Ron Howard, who played Opie on the *Andy Griffith Show* and later starred as Richie on *Happy Days,* is shown with actresses Janet Leigh and Jane Withers. The smile on his face could be acting, but odds are he was enjoying playing with the trains. The show from which this publicity photo came is unknown. Ron Howard went on to become one of the most respected film directors in Hollywood.

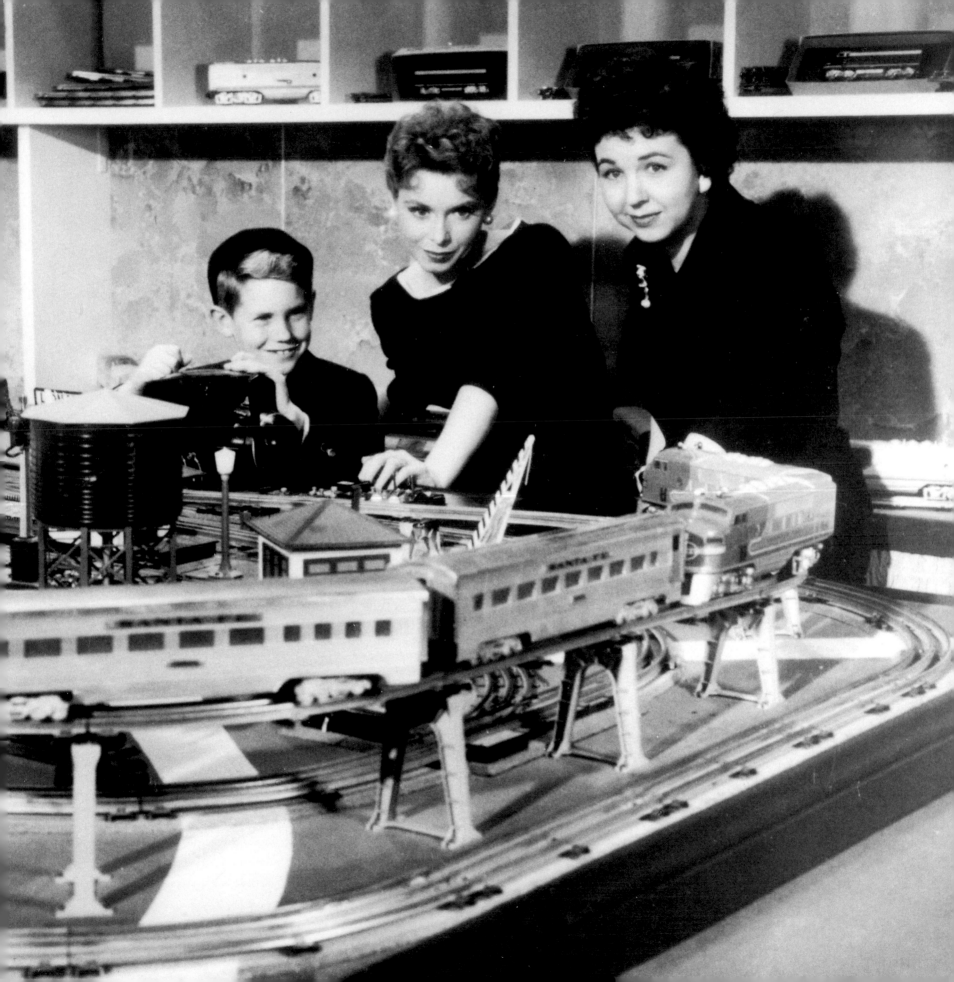

In the fall of 1948, Lionel decided to produce a series of fifteen-minute programs for this new medium. For thirteen Friday evenings, ending just before Christmas, *Tales of the Red Caboose* was broadcast live on an eastern leg of the fledgling ABC network.

The shows revolved around a boy; the layout he had built for his Lionel trains; his doting father; and a grandfatherly neighbor, retired railroad engineer Dan Magee. As the three of them watched the miniature trains,

Engineer Dan would be reminded of exciting railroad stories from his younger days.

Meanwhile, Gilbert American Flyer countered with a similar hastily put-together series of vintage adventures called *The Roar of the Rails*. Apparently, no examples remain of either 1948 series. They were both done live. Television was cumbersome, and the national networks were not yet firmly established.

For years, both Lionel and American Flyer had been encouraging boys who owned their

Recognize James MacArthur, best known in his early adult years as Dano on *Hawaii Five-0*? The man to the right is Art Zirul, employed by Lionel to build display layouts and to serve as technical advisor for television programs that featured Lionel's products.

Wacky band leader Spike Jones, who orchestrated mayhem along with his music by weaving pistol shots, fire sirens, burps, and other outlandish sound effects into his arrangements, is shown in this publicity photo with a 1950s-vintage Lionel Layout.

Local stations in the early days of television had their after-school "heroes." Maybe it was Sheriff Bob or Captain Tom. These themed programs generally consisted of cartoons interspersed with some lessons about life and growing up. Live audiences of children were often part of the show. In Los Angeles the hero was Engineer Bill, host of a program called *Cartoon Express*, sponsored by American Flyer. The photo shows Bill's cohort, Fweight Twain, a.k.a. Wayne Thomas. While sponsorship was undoubtedly expensive, Lionel and Flyer must have believed they were getting their money's worth.

trains to form "model railroad clubs," to pool their resources and increase their enjoyment of the hobby by sharing it with friends. The idea caught on. Any number of boys could get together when the weather was bad, bring their trains, and put up a large layout in attic or basement to while away the hours.

By 1950, ABC, CBS, and NBC had developed coast-to-coast operations, and Lionel was ready to use television in a big way. In a stroke of brilliance, Lionel decided to tie in their trains with another favorite pastime of

school-age boys—baseball! The company hired Joe DiMaggio of the New York Yankees to host the TV series, which was called *The Lionel Clubhouse*. So, whether the viewer thought of a ball club or a model railroad club, it didn't matter—the bases were covered. The thirteen-week Saturday-night-live show premiered on September 23 on NBC.

DiMaggio had long been associated with toy trains. Eleven years before, a picture of him with his Lionel Hudson locomotive had graced the cover of Lionel's *Model Builder*

magazine, so he was, if you pardon the expression, a "natural." And they didn't have to plow under a cornfield to get people to watch. Guests on the show were railroaders and other baseball heroes.

Gilbert American Flyer also capitalized on the club idea, with a show about five boys who operated an elaborate home train layout. *The Boys' Railroad Club* was not done as a live network production, but filmed for broadcast in some sixty markets by local stations. The films ran from

This scene from the popular television series *I Love Lucy* shows the usually harried Ricky (Desi Arnaz) barely escaping being run over by little Ricky's Christmas present. Notice that it's the crack streamliner Santa Fe Warbonnet set. Television exposure like this helped to make that particular locomotive Lionel's top-selling engine. It has been in Lionel's line almost continuously since 1949.

October through December of 1950 and were repeated the next two years. The guests were real railroaders who talked about trains and used the toys to demonstrate their points. Though the term "infomercial" had not yet been coined, the toy train companies certainly did much to pioneer that field.

But Lionel and American Flyer didn't have the production scale or the advertising budgets to use television effectively, so after the initial splash, both companies retreated and

were content to have their products shown occasionally on existing programs.

Payola and plugola were still widely practiced in the industry, so it wasn't difficult to have Lionel trains "placed" on such popular shows as *Arthur Godfrey, Jackie Gleason, I Love Lucy,* and *Kate Smith.* Even many years later, trains were still playing a role on *The Addams Family* and *Captain Kangaroo.*

It's easy to see why toy trains showed up so often on TV in those early years: toy trains were the hottest toys at the time, toy trains

featured lots of motion, and the manufacturers made conscious efforts to place their products on TV.

In those early years, television was still looking for its programming identity, and toy trains offered what they needed. Toy trains and Christmas already had fifty years in which to establish their relationship. So, when Christmas approached, it was only natural that TV executives and writers should think of toy trains.

Ward Kimball spent his professional life as an animator on Walt Disney's best-known film features. He created Jiminy Cricket from *Pinocchio* and the circus train from *Dumbo*. He loved trains of all sizes and shapes and had a full-size, steam-powered railroad, the Grizzly Flats Line, operating on his Orange County, California, property. Ward said that this is where Walt got his idea for steam trains at Disneyland.

Kimball was one of the first to start an organized collection of antique toy trains from all over the world. Housed in two specially constructed buildings behind his home, the extensive collection was displayed by country of origin. One building featured American trains, while the other contained foreign models.

Ward's first train was a Hafner wind-up he got for Christmas when he was nine months old. "My father and uncles bought me toys for my first Christmas that *they* could play with."

Disney animator Ward Kimball had what may have been the finest collection of early foreign and American clockwork and electric toy trains in the world. And it all began with toy trains for Christmas!

Frank Sinatra was undoubtedly the most famous show business celebrity actively involved with toy trains. It is hard to say whether his interest stemmed from childhood, or if his old boss, band leader Tommy Dorsey, had something to do with it. Dorsey had an extensive model railroad in his basement, and both he and Sinatra were frequent visitors to Lionel's New York showroom in the 1940s and 1950s.

Later, "Ol' Blue Eyes" put up a special building on his California estate to house the trains he had collected over the years and an impressive custom-built layout. There was even a winter scene on the upper level, decorated with colored lights—perhaps a nostalgic reminder of Sinatra's boyhood home in Hoboken, New Jersey. In any case, it was probably the only snow in Palm Springs.

Dwight D. Eisenhower, General of the Army and two-term President of the United States, apparently liked trains, too. He is shown at left admiring a layout of shiny, new Marx trains to be presented to his grandson, Dwight David Eisenhower II, on Christmas, 1952. His wife, Mamie, and granddaughter, Susan, also seem to be enjoying the moment.

In less than a month, General Eisenhower would take the oath of office and assume the pressures and responsibilities of the presidency. At this point in time, however, there seems to be nothing but joy, happiness, and—thanks in no small part to Eisenhower himself—peace on earth.

In the photo above, President Eisenhower is being presented with a Lionel model of the famous Civil War locomotive, "The General"—an appropriate gift for the war hero turned peacetime leader.

Richard Kughn's story is literally rags-to-riches. It began with acquiring a Lionel train and culminated with ownership of Lionel Trains Inc. As a seven-year-old Kughn rescued a Lionel train from a garbage can on his way home from school one blustery day in 1936. With the help of his dad, they brought the thing back to life and set it up on a table in the basement. That father-and-son project was the beginning of Kughn's lifelong love of toy trains. His huge collection is one of the finest in the world.

After years of business success in commercial, industrial, and real estate ventures in Detroit, in 1985 Kughn rescued the ailing Lionel train company from the clutches of a conglomerate and ran it himself for a decade.

His personal four-level layout is patterned after the holiday displays often found in department stores during the 1930s, only much bigger. Most of the trains and accessories on it are vintage classics—except for the ones his own company produced.

Now, how did Santa Claus have time to put up this train layout overnight? That seems to be the question four-and-a-half-year-old Karen Ann Yeager is puzzling over on December 25, 1951. Mom is enjoying her daughter's confusion from the kitchen. Karen was born into a toy train family. Her dad, Robert, owned an electric store in Berwick, Pennsylvania, and fixed and sold trains at Christmas time. He built a layout every year that was bigger than the one he built the year before. Eventually he had to add a room onto the house to accommodate the trains. Karen has the trains now and has them running in a newly built room at her house!

Doug Broughman shot this photo of his little brother and sister on Christmas Day, 1959. The Broughmans had played with their dad's childhood Lionel trains before, but at some time between 1955 and 1959, the trains were given to a needy family. The new trains in this photo, headed up by a flashy orange, black, and white New Haven diesel locomotive, belong to little brother Steve (age seven). Sister Cathy, age five and in the middle of the action, mugs for the camera. Steve, now with the tremendous responsibility of hauling freight over his railroad, takes the situation much more seriously.

Graham Claytor's hobby intersected with his professional career in a number of ways. No stranger to the real world of transportation, he served as vice president and general counsel to the Southern Railway, as Secretary of the Navy in the Carter administration, and for a time as president of Amtrak, the national railroad passenger corporation.

The late Mr. Claytor began collecting obscure antique toy trains in the 1950s, when the acquisition of legendary early-twentieth-century items by Boucher, Carlisle & Finch, and Voltamp was still possible. The products of these manufacturers make up the bulk of the collection.

Mr. Claytor's stunning antique train collection provides a perfect example of how an array of colorful collectibles can become an integral part of the interior décor of a home. Fortunately, Mr. Claytor's spacious Georgetown house had many built-in bookcases throughout, which were easily converted into display shelves.

Ed Dougherty, PGA Senior Tour golfer, was given a Lionel *Texas Special* locomotive for Christmas when he was a boy. He still has it and has been accumulating toy trains almost ever since. His vast collection of post-World War II Lionel trains, accessories, and displays is one of the finest and most extensive in the world.

As a regular on the pro circuit since 1975, Ed has traveled all over the country, ostensibly to play in tournaments, but finding enough time to scour hobby shops and other locales in search of trains. He knows practically every hobby shop in all the major cities on the tour. During the short off-season, he even finds time to enjoy his collection!

In addition to the regular sets, Dougherty has many rare, one-of-a-kind items as well as hard-to-find store display layouts, posters, and related retail paraphernalia in the special two-story, environmentally controlled building he erected to provide a safe home for his collection.

Still actively pursuing the hobby, Ed says he'll give up train collecting when the fun stops. So far, that hasn't happened.

What a wonderful snapshot of an American family Christmas! Seven-year-old W. J. Edwards gazes intently at his new train on Christmas morning of 1937. His expression is a little serious, but Bill insists he was happy with his new gift. He recalls that he used to enjoy "running the engine into Lincoln Log barriers." Bill's older sister, Jeanette, in her satin dress, sits primly on the chair. To the right is younger brother Jon, not yet old enough to play with electric trains.

Gene Brez got his first train on Christmas Day of 1937. In 1941, when the photo at right was taken, Gene had an elaborate layout, complete with tunnel, signal, grade crossing flasher, cast-metal soldiers, and a teddy bear. The same trains circle Gene's tree today.

Toy Trains Yesterday, Today, and Perhaps Tomorrow

For decades—especially throughout the 1930s, '40s, and 50's —electric trains were at the top of every little boy's (and some girls') list for Santa. By the early 1960s, however, Christmas dreams were changing. Other interactive electronic toys, such as slot cars and computer games, took over the kids' "most wanted" lists. With the diminished demand for Christmas trains, the interest in holiday layouts also ebbed. Those traditional displays that remained in the 1960s and '70s were running on the momentum of nostalgia, largely perpetuated by parents who had grown up playing with trains under the tree.

This trend reflected what was happening in the toy train industry generally at the same time. Marketing strategies changed as the manufacturers began targeting adults. Instead of encouraging children to pester their parents for a train, the catalog sales pitches were directed at parents, who had a more-or-less sacred obligation to introduce their children to the joys associated with toy trains, all in the name of wholesome fun and family togetherness.

Quite a few fathers refused to give up their childhood love of toy trains, clinging to the fondest memories of their childhood. Now in a financial position to acquire the trains they only dreamed of owning as kids, they fulfilled their fantasies by haunting flea markets, garage sales, and hobby shops in search of toy trains that others had discarded or chosen to liquidate. Many put together large collections of their own favorite childhood trains. Others built elaborate model railroad layouts on which to operate their toy trains and accessories in a somewhat realistic setting. These new train collectors and operators even managed to keep Lionel afloat during the lean transitional years.

A strong influx of Baby Boomers, who had children of their own by the 1980s, made the hobby healthy again. By their sheer numbers, they created a demand that turned things around for the existing manufacturers and encouraged other companies to enter the field. The renaissance was under way. Today, we have more excellent-quality, technologically sophisticated toy trains on the market than ever before. The choices are almost limitless and there are price points and ranges for every budget.

In retrospect, it perhaps was the introduction of Large Scale trains from LGB (Lehmann Gross Bahn) in the 1980s that made having trains circling the Christmas tree popular again. The LGB models of European prototypes were whimsical and toylike to American eyes. They ran quietly and well for extended periods of time without attention or service, making them perfect for hours of running under the tree. Many adults bought them for just that purpose. The LGB marketing strategy encouraged this. These charming trains were sold in more places than the usual hobby and toy stores. Upscale specialty and gift shops, as well as interior and furniture retailers, used them in home-style Christmas tree displays with excellent results.

So, in the past twenty years, having a toy train under the Christmas tree has been elevated from something intended to please the kids to an essential element in holiday decoration that seems to have no age (or gender) limitation. More and more trains appear in this context every year, even in homes without children.

At Christmastime, toy trains pop up in advertising campaigns of all kinds, particularly where a warm home environment is depicted. Corporate America has recognized that Americans respond to appeals that are nostalgia-driven. And it's not only commercials. Even the back bar of the NBC *Today* news set in 2001 had a tree, a row of poinsettias, an assortment of wooden Nutcracker figures, and a highly stylized toy train pulled by a big red steam locomotive.

By every indication, the long-established tie between the toy train and Christmas is alive, well, probably stronger than ever, and not just for kids any more. That speaks volumes about the future. Regardless of what trendy toy might be "in" for any given Christmas, in some form, a toy train will likely be a part of the scene, running round and round and round beneath the tree.

Selected Toy Train Reading

World's Greatest Toy Train Maker, by Roger Carp

Lionel's Model Builder: *The Magazine That Shaped the Toy Train Hobby,* by Terry Thompson and Roger Carp

Classic Lionel Display Layouts You Can Build, by Roger Carp

How to Build Your First Lionel Layout, by Stan Trzoniec

Introduction to Toy Train Collecting and Operating, by John Grams

Greenberg's Pocket Price Guides
    Lionel Trains 1901-2003
    American Flyer 1946-2003
    Marx Trains: 8th Edition

Greenberg' Guide to Lionel Trains 1987-1995: The Richard Kughn Era, by Michael Solly

Greenberg's Guide to Lionel Trains 1901-1942 Volume II: O and OO Gauges, by Bruce Greenberg

Greenberg' Guide to Lionel Trains 1945-1969 Volume I: Motive Power and Rolling Stock, by Paul Ambrose

Classic Toy Trains magazine, Kalmbach Publishing Co.

All of the above titles are available from Kalmbach Publishing Co., 21027 Crossroads Circle, Waukesha, WI 53186; 1-800-533-6644; secure online ordering available at http://kalmbachbooks.com

Photo and Art Credits

Most of the black-and-white photos in this book were supplied by readers of *Classic Toy Trains* magazine. The majority of the color photos were taken by Kalmbach staff editors and photographers: William Zuback, James Forbes, Rebecca Saliture, Darla Evans, Andy Sperandeo, and Chris Becker. Other credits are as follows:

Angela Trotta Thomas, 20, 48, 72, 94; Robert Sherman, 56; Gary Linden, 59; George Lindgren, 61, 108; Mike Matejka, 66; *Press-Intelligencer* collection, Seattle Museum of History and Industry, 67; Robert James, 68; George Hall, 68, 69, 76; Robert Diamante, 74, 75; Fritz von Tagen, 78-83; Bill Novak, 89, 93; courtesy Arthur Zirul, 92, 138; Jim Flynn, 102; Steve Schaffer, 112; Scott Wallace, 116; Paul Dolkos, 127; Dave Frary, 128.

If you enjoyed *Toy Train Memories* and would like to see your own photos in a future book about toy trains and children, send copies of your photos (not the originals) to:
    Kalmbach Books
    Kalmbach Publishing Co.
    21027 Crossroads Circle
    Waukesha, WI 53187

Index to Those Whose Toy Train Memories We've Shared

| John and Rob Romagna, Christmas morning 1949